D1418207

DATE DUE			
		DISCARD	

We the People

A REVOLUTIONARY IDEA

Alexander Hamilton and James Madison

by Paul J. Deegan

Abdo & Daughters
Minneapolis

Published by Abdo & Daughters, 6537 Cecilia Circle, Bloomington, Minnesota 55435

Library bound edition distributed by Rockbottom Books, Pentagon Tower, P.O. Box 36036, Minneapolis, Minnesota 55435

Library of Congress Number: 87-071092   ISBN: 0-939179-20-2

Cover illustration by Elaine Wadsworth

Consultants:

Phyllis R. Abbott
Ph.D. — University of Wisconsin (Madison)
Professor of History
Mankato State University
Mankato, Minnesota

Bailey W. Blethen
J.D. — University of Minnesota Law School
Partner in law firm of Blethen, Gage & Krause
Mankato, Minnesota

Lewis H. Croce
Ph.D. — University of Maryland
Professor of History
Mankato State University
Mankato, Minnesota

Table of Events

First Continental Congress Convenes	Philadelphia	September 5, 1774
Battle of Lexington and Concord	Massachusetts	April 19,1775
Vote by Second Continental Congress on Independence	Philadelphia	July 2, 1776
Signing of Declaration of Independence by President of Second Continental Congress	Philadelphia	July 4, 1776
Articles of Confederation Ratified		March 1, 1781
Mount Vernon Conference	Virginia	March 24-28, 1785
Annapolis Convention	Maryland	September 11-14, 1786
Constitutional Convention Convenes	Philadelphia	May 25, 1787
The Constitution of the United States of America Signed	Philadelphia	September 17, 1787

"We the People of the United States . . .
establish this CONSTITUTION for the United
States of America."

One was a man who made his way to a leadership role after coming to this country in his late teens. The other was a man born to wealth who spent much of his life in government.

Two unlikely allies, Alexander Hamilton and James Madison, played leading roles in the birth and delivery of the United States Constitution.

Hamilton's feisty, confident manner ensured that he would have enemies. He died from a pistol wound inflicted by one of them. Madison quietly, smoothly brought others around to seeing things his way. He died peacefully on his Virginia estate.

In the year 1787, it was another man, however, who was probably the best known person in the new nation called the United States of America. George Washington had been a hero in the war fought to gain

Alexander Hamilton

James Madison

independence from England — the Revolutionary War.

Later, he would be the first president of the United States. He would be known as the "Father of the Country."

In 1787 Washington was 55 years old. He had retired from public life, so he thought, four years earlier. He had been enjoying the life of a gentleman farmer on his Mount Vernon Plantation.

Mount Vernon was in the northeastern part of Virginia not far from present day Washington, D.C. That city, which did not exist in 1787, would become the future capitol of the nation and would be named for George Washington.

Washington in 1787 was not only famous, he also was one of the most respected men in the country. He had been asked by the state of Virginia to be one of its delegates to a meeting to be held in Philadelphia in May 1787.

When it became known he was willing to go to Philadelphia, the meeting took on more importance in the minds of many other leaders of the young nation.

No one knew it that spring, but the meeting was to produce another revolution. The meeting would not produce another war. It would produce an idea — a revolutionary idea.

Now Washington was leaving Mount Vernon to go to Philadelphia. The trip was less than 175 miles. It would take Washington five days to make the trip in a horse-driven carriage!

Today in five hours we can travel from New York to California. But there were no jet airplanes 200 years ago. We can make a 175-mile trip by car over paved roads in less than four hours. But there were no automobiles nor paved roads in 1787. The 200-mile trip from Boston to New York by stagecoach took a week!

General George Washington's Carriage

Today airplanes cross the Atlantic Ocean in five hours. That same trip had taken 49 days in 1785! That was how long Benjamin Franklin's ocean voyage took when he returned from Europe. Franklin, too, was a delegate to the meeting in Philadelphia, where he lived.

Philadelphia was the country's largest city in 1787. It was a busy river port of some 40,000 people. Many shopkeepers and craftsmen had moved there. It was also a Quaker city. It was also to be for a time the capital of the United States under the Constitution.

New York City was the nation's capital when the Constitution went into effect. Congress voted in 1790 to locate the capital in Philadelphia for 10 years when it would be moved to its present location on the banks of the Potomac River. Thus, Washington would return to Philadelphia to serve his two terms as President.

As were other large cities at the time, Philadelphia was dirty, smelly, and noisy. Horses were the major means of transportation if you did not walk. There weren't even any bicycles then.

It's hard to believe how different things were 200 years ago!

There were only the 13 original states. Georgia was both the furthest west and the furthest south. The nation, however, also included the Northwest Territory. The area which later became the eastern part of the state of Minnesota was the western edge of this territory. However, white men were then living further to the west and north in what would become Minnesota.

There were less than 4 million people in the 13 states in 1787. Today there are some 240 million in 50 states.

Ninety out of every 100 persons were engaged in farming in 1787. Today only about 2 of 100 farm.

Communication was slow in the 1780s. Not only was there no television, there was no radio or telephone. There was not even photography. Today TV cameras can show you instantly what's happening almost anywhere in the world. In the 1780s news traveled slowly, even within a state.

We know today how very important the meeting in Philadelphia was to be in the history of the United States. Yet the meeting attracted little attention in 1787. Most Americans did not know that it was taking place.

And they didn't learn anything about it while it was being held. The delegates ruled that they would do their work in absolute secrecy.

The meeting in Philadelphia we now call the Constitution Convention. However, as we shall see, the men — no women participated — who took part in that meeting were not called together to write a new constitution.

But they did.

The original Constitution — it was to be amended 26 times by 1987 — was the product of 55 men from 12 states. Rhode Island sent no delegates to the convention.

The delegates worked for four months over the summer of 1787. Not all 55 were there the entire time. The delegates discussed, argued, and debated all through the summer. When they finished in September, they called their work a "Constitution for the United States of America."

Some say that document signed in September 1787 is the most important document ever written.

Historians call it a "living document." They mean that it lives and impacts the present. It affects our lives today, 200 years after it was written.

How unusual is the U.S. Constitution?

Some 160 nations have constitutions today. All but 14 of them have been adopted since 1945.

Two of every three of these constitutions have been either adopted or revised in the last 17 years.

Over half the world's independent nations have had more than one constitution since 1945.

However, that remarkable document produced 200 years ago in Philadelphia remans this nation's guiding force.

It is the world's oldest written constitution in use.

The original document is four pages long. It has 4,543 words, including the signers' names. It was written in the formal style of the time. It contains words and phrases which appear strange to us today. Despite its dated style and language, we look upon it as the cornerstone of our democratic republic.

A revolutionary idea was nurtured in Philadelphia 200 years ago. That idea was that the people will determine who will govern them!

How that idea took root and was given life isn't how you might imagine it happened. How the Constitution came to be is a story of events and people. It is also one of history's most dramatic examples of political compromise.

The events were both recent and long ago.

The more recent ones included the birth of the new nation, the United States of America. Its birthday was

July 4, 1776. On that day the Declaration of Independence was approved in Philadelphia by the Second Continental Congress.

This Congress first met in Philadelphia on May 10, 1775. A First Continental Congress had met in the fall of 1774 in the same city.

The Second Continental Congress had adopted a resolution on May 10, 1776, favoring permanent governments in each of the 13 colonies. On June 7, Richard Henry Lee of Virginia put forward a resolution calling for independence from Great Britain for the colonies. It also called for a general confederation of the colonies. It permitted establishing relations with foreign countries.

On July 2, 12 of the colonies adopted the resolution calling for independence. All 13 colonies were represented at the Congress. But New York did not okay the resolution until July 9, after it was in effect.

The president of the Continental Congress, John Hancock, signed the Declaration of Independence on July 4. On August 19, those members of Congress in Philadelphia at the time gathered around a table in the State House to sign a copy of the document. Fifty-five men added their signatures to that of Hancock.

Eleven years later, eight of the signers would be delegates to the Constitutional Convention. Six of them would sign the Constitution in the same State House, which we now call Independence Hall.

The writing of the Declaration of Independence was largely the work of another Virginian. Thomas Jefferson, then 33, was one of five men appointed to draft a statement. Their task included explaining the decision of the colonies to declare themselves free of English rule.

Jefferson was asked to write this document because he was considered to have an appealing style of writing.

The document he wrote was applauded as the sign of a new political age. It hailed liberty and self-government.

The Declaration of Independence stated that all men have equal and God-given rights. Citizens no longer would be subject to the power of a king.

This was the revolutionary idea to which it gave birth.

Eleven years later, this principle was strengthened by the Constitution. The Constitution forbid the government to grant titles of nobility. There would be no king's men in the United States.

One particular king was especially unpopular in the new nation. King George III of Great Britain had had been somewhat less than thrilled that his colonies across the ocean intended to establish their own nation.

Britain even had soldiers in America to protect its interest in what the king viewed as the "New" England. The colonial leaders had been unhappy for some time with the controls placed on them by Britain. Merchants and planters, in particular, were unhappy. The discontent had produced some protests in Massachusetts.

In 1774 George III and the British Parliament decided they were going to show the colonists who was boss. Early in 1775, the British House of Commons declared Massachusetts to be in a state of rebellion. The British were ready to use force if necessary to hold on to their colonies in America. That decision eventually led to fighting.

The first conflict between British soldiers and colonial militiamen took place in Massachusetts in 1775. Eight Americans were killed on April 19 in fighting at Lexington and Concord near Boston. The Revolutionary War was underway.

Thus, the fighting had begun before the Second Continental Congress held its first session in Philadelphia on May 10.

In June Congress had created the Continental Army. Guess who had been everyone's choice to be commander-in-chief of the army? George Washington had taken command on the third day of July.

The Continental Army fought the British for another six years. It would be eight years before the war was officially over. At one time the second floor of Independence Hall was a temporary prison for captured Continental soldiers. While British soldiers occupied Philadelphia in the winter of 1777-1778,

Washington's battered army camped nearby at Valley Forge.

But also in 1778, France joined forces with the colonists. Three years later, in October 1781, over 7,000 British soldiers surrendered to Continental Army and French forces at Yorktown in southeast Virginia. The fighting was over except for some occasional skirmishes.

The official end of the war came two years later with the signing in 1783 of the Treaty of Paris. Great Britain recognized the independence of the colonies and granted to them the territory between the Appalachian Mountains and the Mississippi river.

The 13 former British colonies were now officially the United States of America.

Free they were. United they were not.

There was no strong central government. General Washington had complained about this during the Revolutionary War. He believed the new nation needed a federal government with powers over the states. That view was held even more strongly by his wartime confidential assistant, a young captain named Alexander Hamilton.

Hamilton and Washington had little in common, yet became friends.

Washington, a native Virginian, was 43 when he took command of the Continental Army. Known and respected throughout the colonies, he was not one to take hasty action. He was a skilled politician and had a reputation of being able to identify and define a problem. It was said of him that "when hearing all suggestions, he selected whatever was best." He also got high marks for his honesty and fairness.

Hamilton was only 20 when the war began. He had only been in the country for two years. He had been born in the West Indies. He was brilliant — he had studied at King's College in New York City (the present Columbia University). After the fighting ended, he would become a lawyer after studying for only three months. He would also marry into the upper level of New York society. He would found the Bank of New York.

Years later he would serve as Secretary of the Treasury. And he, as was his son, was shot to death in a duel — a prearranged formal combat between two persons held to settle a point of honor.

Hamilton was to be a major player in the development of the U.S. Constitution. In fact, he is generally credited with being the one person most responsible for the calling of the Constitutional Convention.

He began this mission while serving with Washington by urging the general to speak out in regard to changing the way the nation was governed.

During the war, Hamilton wrote a very long letter to a friend in September 1780. He put in writing the need for action. You can't govern through 13 states, he wrote. He decried Congress' lack of power. He said there was "only one remedy — to call a convention of all the states." First, however, he said people should be prepared "by sensible and popular writing."

Throughout most of the war, the country's only governing body was the Second Continental Congress, which continued in existence.

In 1776 the Articles of Confederation were drafted in this Congress. This 13-article document was approved and sent to the states for their approval in November 1777. It took until 1781 for all the states to give their approval. The country then operated under these Articles.

Though the 13 former colonies acted as a nation in fighting the English, the Articles of Confederation really did not form a nation. They created "a firm league of friendship." The Articles formed a detached league of states. They did provide a forum in which the states could cooperate. They could defend themselves. They could trade with each other. Under the Articles, the United States could send representatives to other nations.

The Articles did not create a strong federal government. Each state was still independent. The members of the Second Continental Congress did not want a strong national government. The loyalties they felt were toward their respective states. They were ready to throw off the rule of a powerful king. They did not want to create a new central authority with power over all of them.

Therefore, in the 1780s each state operated like a small country. Each had written its own constitution. A state cooperated with another state only if it chose to do so. It had become clear that the Articles of Confederation weren't working.

There were several major problems. These included foreign trade, trade between the states, and the absence of a national system of money.

European countries would not enter agreements with the United States to buy and sell goods. They knew Congress could not make a state honor any agreement.

Trade between the states themselves was a problem because states taxed and controlled each other's goods.

The nation was practically broke. Since no federal money could be issued, states issued their own paper money, which usually was worthless.

Also, the Congress established under the Articles of Confederation was slowly withering away. By 1786 there were seldom enough Congressmen on hand in New York City to conduct business. That summer it ceased to function.

The new nation's problems were widely recognized. However, every effort to enact changes failed. Any change in the Articles of Confederation had to win the agreement of every state.

Despite the lack of response to efforts to amend the Articles, Hamilton never stopped trying. He was not a member of the New York legislature, yet in 1782 he convinced that body to pass a resolution urging a meeting to deal with the problems. That same year he was elected to Congress. He drafted a similar proposal, but it was not enacted.

Those men — called nationalists — who favored a stronger national government were taking a position that at the time was a radical one.

It was a revolutionary idea that loyalty to the new nation rises above state loyalties.

They came to this viewpoint partly through disappointment. The founders of the country had wanted a different and better system of government. They had not liked the way they had been governed by the king and the British Parliament when the states had been British colonies. They also opposed a government whose authority came from a church.

The founders had led the breakaway from Great Britain. They had new ideas. They had been excited about following a new path. They knew the seed of a revolutionary idea had been planted.

The founders were part of a small group of people

involved in political decision making before, during, and after the birth of the United States.

Some had been involved in creating the new nation. Many had fought against Britain in the Revolutionary War. Many were active in state governments. Some had served in the Confederation Congress. Several would be delegates to the Constitutional Convention.

The first presidents of the United States would come from this group.

These men were not a formal group. But they were part of a privileged class. They had money and were members of the upper social class. One of these leaders described this group as "the better class of people."

Many of these men also were "intellectuals" — intelligent, educated, well-read, thoughtful men.

In the 1780s, these leaders once again began studying the form of government they wanted for the United States. They increased their reading. They read or reread classical political writings. They read the latest European political thought. They sought books about republics.

Two of these young American intellectuals found themselves separated by the Atlantic Ocean.

One was James Madison. A native Virginian in his mid-30s, Madison's family was well-to-do. He had been a member of Congress from 1779 through 1783.

He also would be a delegate to the meeting in Philadelphia.

A small man, 5 feet 4, who spoke quietly, Madison is known as the "Father of the Constitution." As Hamilton is credited with leading the call for the Constitutional Convention, Madison is most identified with the document produced in Philadelphia.

His "Notes on the Federal Constitution" is the only full record of what took place during the Constitutional Convention. However, they were not published until Madison's death nearly 50 years later.

With Hamilton and John Jay, Madison wrote a series of letters to newspapers under the name the *Federalist Papers*. Many believe even today that the *Federalist Papers* are the most authentic explanation of our constitutional system.

A man who pursued his goals, Madison could also be flexible, a quality that was to be important in Philadelphia during the summer of 1787.

Madison would later be Secretary of State and the fourth President of the United States.

While serving in the Virginia legislature, Madison had met Thomas Jefferson. The two men had become close friends and remained life-long allies. They would found the Democratic party, called Democratic-Republican at the time.

Jefferson, older by eight years, was in Paris in the

mid-1780s. He was the American Minister to France. He began this assignment in 1784 and would not return to America until 1789.

Also a native of Virginia, Jefferson was a lawyer and planter. He had gone to college in Virginia at William and Mary. He would be the nation's third President. Madison was his Secretary of State.

While Jefferson was in France, Madison and he wrote back and forth. Madison asked his friend to send him books which "may throw light on" the governments of other countries.

Jefferson sent books from Paris — by the trunkload. He sent Madison hundreds of books.

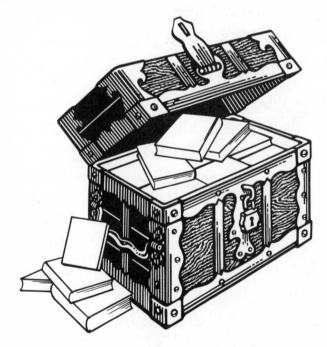

As a result, it has been said that Madison was the delegate best prepared intellectually to go to Philadelphia.

The unrest felt by the nation's political leaders was also felt by the average citizen. While men like Washington, Hamilton, Madison, and Jefferson were concerned, others, particularly merchants and small farmers, were hurting.

Merchants could not pay their debts — most of which were to British suppliers. Debts incurred to finance the war by Congress and the states went unpaid. As a result debtors were demanding that the states issue large amounts of paper money. Several did. The money lost its value, and creditors were then unhappy.

Massachusetts was one state facing a large debt. Massachusetts legislators decided to try to pay off the debt by enacting more taxes. These new taxes hit hard on small farmers. Most of them lived west of Boston in the interior of the state.

These farmers were having a hard time making it before the added taxes. They seldom had any money. They often exchanged their crop for food or clothing. Now the state wanted more money from them.

Massachusetts' legal system was another problem. It was developed much earlier and had not been changed to keep abreast of times. The system required almost everything to be officially recorded — for a fee. The fees weren't high, but few farmers had any cash. Again, the small farmer was hit hard.

The farmers of western Massachusetts were angry and frustrated. They were fiercely independent men. Now, however, they were hurting enough to band together. Armed groups began gathering at the place where a local court was to be in session. They prevented the courts from meeting. The court shutdowns began in 1786 and continued into the following year.

These actions frightened not only the judges, the armed protests scared other government officials and the Boston merchants.

There were, however, some in Boston who sought to take advantage of the unrest. These were men who had liked being under British rule. Some of them actually wanted the new nation to fail so that the British would return. Now these men saw a chance to weaken the state government. So they provided financial support to better organize the protestors.

This meant protestors got paid for drilling with their weapons. But as time passed and they weren't called to action, the leaders of the groups in training became impatient . . . and afraid. The threat they represented to the state probably was overemphasized by state officials. Nonetheless, Massachusetts officials ordered the arrest of some of the group leaders.

One of those group leaders was a former captain in the Continental Army named Daniel Shays. On an extremely cold day in late January 1787, Shays found himself in charge of some 1,200 armed men waiting outside Springfield, Massachusetts. They were waiting to move into Springfield to get more weapons. They intended to capture the Springfield arsenal.

Things had gotten out of hand as far as Shays was concerned. He was now a frightened, confused man. He was expecting another group of armed men to meet him in Springfield when he marched his men into town on January 25. However, no help appeared, but the state militia was waiting for the protestors. The government soldiers opened fire on Shays' group. The first volley killed four men. The rest fled. Shays' "Rebellion" was over.

In reality, so were the protest actions of all the rebellious farmers.

However, the story of the protests was big news in the other states. The protests in Massachusetts emphasized problems being faced throughout the country. The threat of armed rebellion alarmed leaders elsewhere. They worried that what took place in Massachusetts might happen in their states. They saw the protests as a threat to the nation's ability to govern itself.

This threat strengthened the convictions of those who favored a stronger national government. However, it would be one thing to make the national government strong enough to be able to squash a rebellion by makeshift soldiers. It would be more difficult to address the problems which led to the revolt in Massachusetts. And problems relating to finance, taxes, trade, and commerce existed in the other 12 states as well.

It was more and more clear that the national government established by the Articles of Confederation could not respond to these problems.

Still many state legislators feared and opposed attempts to establish a real national government. In 1785, for instance, some Massachusetts politicians blocked their own legislature's call for a general convention to revise the Articles.

However, in 1785 Virginia and Maryland had taken what would turn out to be the first major step on the road to a Constitutional Convention.

MARYLAND

Potomac River

VIRGINIA

MOUNT VERNON CONFERENCE
March 24-28, 1785

The two states had agreed to settle a dispute over fishing and shipping rights on waterways including the Potomac River. This river was a boundary between the two states.

Rivers were the highways of the 1780s. There were no good roads, so the major means of transporting goods was by water.

Delegates from the two states had been invited by George Washington to meet at his home in Mount Vernon.

Washington had more than a passing interest in the dispute. He was considering starting a company that would link the Potomac with the Ohio River by canals. He owned 10,000 acres along the Ohio River. The canals would open up trade to what is now the Midwest. He expected this would be a very profitable business.

The bistate agreement actually flouted the Confederate Congress because the two states made an interstate compact outside the structure of the Articles of Confederation.

The five delegates at The Mount Vernon Conference also went a step further than settling their dispute. They developed ideas for solving broader problems concerning trade between states. This added step would be the path that led to the Constitutional Convention.

In January 1786 the Virginia legislature asked that all the states be invited to a meeting to consider interstate trade problems. A month later, Governor Patrick Henry of Virginia wrote all the other governors asking them to send delegates to a commercial convention to be held in Annapolis, Maryland, on the first day of September.

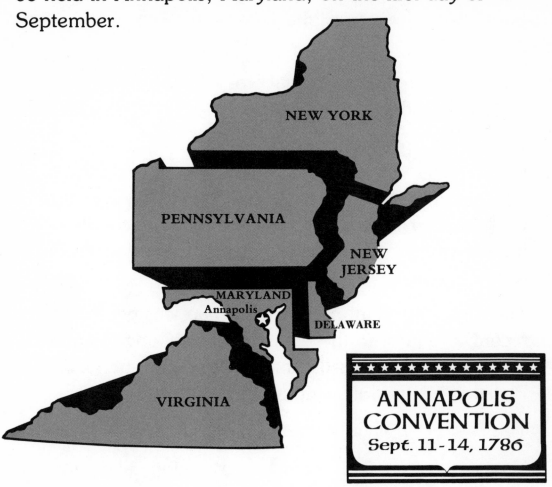

NEW YORK

PENNSYLVANIA

NEW JERSEY

MARYLAND
Annapolis

DELAWARE

VIRGINIA

★★★★★★★★★★★★★★★
ANNAPOLIS
CONVENTION
Sept. 11-14, 1786

Nine states chose delegates. Four states did not act on the invitation. Meanwhile, there was talk, even by Congressmen, of giving up on the idea of a union and perhaps trying to form regional groupings of states.

Those who not only wanted to keep a united nation but to strengthen the union also heard this talk. They came to Annapolis in September prepared.

The Annapolis convention opened on September 11, 1786. As expected, many delegates did not show up. There were only 12 men from five states — Delaware,

New Jersey, New York, Pennsylvania, and Virginia. There were none from the host state.

There were not enough delegates for a quorum. But, some historians believe, that was what some who were there had anticipated.

A small group of ardent nationalists had come prepared. Madison and Hamilton were among them. These men had no intention of allowing a quorum to be present. They wanted only to meet and then say that attempts to change the Articles of Confederation weren't going to work.

The most important part of their plan was get on record a request to the Confederation Congress and the states that a Constitutional Convention be held in Philadelphia the following May.

This is exactly what happened.

Hamilton, of course, wrote the resolution calling for the Philadelphia convention. Adopted September 14, it called for delegates to the Philadelphia meeting the following spring "to take into consideration the trade and commerce of the United States." It also said the delegates were to consider "the situation of the United States" and "devise such further provisions as shall appear to them necessary. . .".

By the time Shays' men were routed at Springfield four months later, five states had voted to send delegates to Philadelphia. They were Virginia, New Jersey, Pennsylvania, North Carolina, and Delaware.

Virginia was first, and it's selection of George Washington as a delegate was not accidental. His selection lended prestige to the proposed convention and influenced other states to agree to take part.

Massachusetts and New York selected delegates soon after the incident at Springfield. In April, Georgia and South Carolina named delegates. Connecticut and Maryland did not name delegates until May, the month the convention was to begin. New Hampshire did not get around to doing so until June when the convention was already underway. Of the 13 states, only Rhode Island refused to take part in the Constitutional Convention.

Meanwhile, the Confederation Congress had also approved the Philadelphia meeting. But it had done so hesitantly. One Congressman said such a convention had no right to suggest changes in the nation's laws.

On February 21 the Confederation Congress had finally voted to ask the states to send delegates to Philadelphia. However, Congress was definitely not suggesting a new constitution. It said the "sole and express purpose" of the Philadelphia meeting was to be one of "revising the Articles of Confederation."

The Constitutional Convention was critical in terms of saving what the country's founders thought they had established — a republic. However, as historians have pointed out, the meeting in Philadelphia would not make much difference in the immediate future for most Americans then alive.

It is doubtful that any of the delegates who came to Philadelphia in 1787 were looking ahead 200 years. But many, Washington among them, were concerned about the future. These men were not limiting their viewpoint. They wanted a united nation.

Washington was on record as saying that more than tinkering was needed to make effective national laws. He also had said he did not think "we can exist long as a nation" without a central government with authority over the states.

When the day came that the convention was supposed to begin, a rainy May 14, only two delegates had arrived in Philadelphia, Madison, always wanting to be prepared, came 11 days early. He had come down from New York City. He and some of the other delegates were members of the Confederation Congress, which continued in session during the Constitutional Convention.

The early arrivers found that workers had put gravel on the cobblestone streets near Independence Hall. This was done to reduce the noise from horses passing near the plain brick building.

The Constitutional Convention got underway May 25 when a quorum was present. From then until mid-September, 55 delegates would be on hand at one time or another.

The delegates met six days a week, usually from 11 a.m. to 3 p.m. The average daily attendance was 30.

Some delegates attended every session. Others left and returned. Thirteen left for good, nine for personal reasons and four because they disagreed with what was taking place.

New Hampshire's delegates didn't get to Philadelphia until July 23 because there had been no funds to pay their expenses.

A total of 74 delegates had been appointed by the 12 states. Five did not believe the meeting should be held. Among them was Virginia's Henry who said he "smelled a rat." Illness prevented 14 others from coming.

The delegates were representative of the decision-makers in the new nation — white, male, Protestants with above-average incomes. Some were wealthy.

At the time, most white, male Americans were small farmers. None of the 55 delegates who would attend the Constitutional Convention belonged to that group. Twenty-two are said to have had considerable income from agriculture. However, most of these were Southern planters who owned slaves. There were wealthy Northern farmers and some who owned country estates.

The delegates in Philadelphia were not strangers to government. Forty-six of them had been members of state legislatures. Thirty-four were lawyers. Thirty-three had served in the Revolutionary War. Twenty-seven were college graduates.

Their average age was 44. Benjamin Franklin at 81 was the oldest. Jonathan Dayton from New Jersey was the youngest at 26.

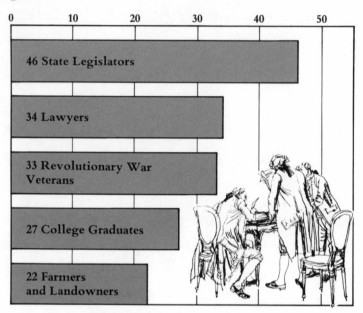

55 DELEGATES TO THE CONSTITUTIONAL CONVENTION
May 25 – Sept. 17, 1787

When the delegates finished their work in Philadelphia, they would continue to be leaders. Two as we have seen would be President of the United States. One would become Vice President. Four would serve in the Cabinet. Fourteen would be senators and five would be elected to the House of Representatives. Twelve would be state governors.

In 1987 the United States celebrates the 200th anniversary of the document written by these men in Philadelphia. One of the words that comes to most

government bonds. Twenty-four were money lenders. Several owned land in the Western territories.

That the Constitution, when written, protected ownership of property, required the federal government to pay off the bonds, and backed up contracts was no accident.

The framers took care of these things, but did not believe that people unlike them with no property, little education, and no ties to the upper levels of society should have much opportunity to participate in governing the United States.

And these people didn't, for the most part, when the framers completed their work in Philadelphia. Under the original Constitution, no one could vote who didn't already have that right before the delegates came to Independence Hall. Left intact were existing state requirements about who was eligible to vote.

The original Constitution excluded women from participating in democracy. It gave no rights to the 700,000 black slaves then living in the United States. Slaves were considered to be property. Native Americans ("Indians") did not benefit from the document finished in September 1787.

There was no bill of rights in the original Constitution. It was brought up at the last moment, but voted down 10 states to none. Delegates from two states had left before the vote was taken. Rhode Island, of course, was never represented in Philadelphia.

So the original Constitution provided little in the way of rights, except for property rights. But what about democracy?

The Constitution established a system of representative democracy. This means people elect someone to represent and govern them. Decisions are made by the elected representatives.

Direct democracy is people participating directly in every decision of the government. It was the system followed at New England town meetings before the Revolutionary War. However, direct democracy is not very practical. It means getting everybody together to discuss and vote on each proposed change.

We know the framers didn't want to bother with anything like that. One delegate in Philadelphia, Connecticut's Roger Sherman, said:

"The people immediately should have as little to do as may be about the government." He said the people lack "information and are constantly liable to be misled."

Given the attitude of the framers, how did the Constitution end up providing the nation with a democracy.

The framers may have been snobs, but they weren't stupid. They were also politicians. They both represented their states and had a goal to accomplish.

That goal was to solve the problems which had arisen

from trying to operate as a nation under the Articles of Confederation. The nationalists among the delegates saw a much stronger central government as the answer.

All the framers wanted to avoid what they had once known — total power in one person who ruled for life, a king. They wanted a more stable union. They wanted contracts which were enforceable. They sought a sound financial base for the country.

The delegates debated how this could be achieved. Discussion was sometimes heated. The convention had been closed to the public and the press of the day so that opinions could be expressed freely. Sentries marched outside the State House so no one could listen at the windows. There were no official notes taken at the sessions.

The delegates discussed their ideas under the watchful eye of Washington. Not surprisingly, he had been everyone's choice to be president of the convention. His views were well known and he stayed out of the debates at the meetings. He did consult in private with delegates.

Although Hamilton gets paramount credit for bringing about the convention, he was not a major factor in drafting the Constitution. He stated his views, but lacked the political savy of Madison and others. Hamilton actually went home for about six weeks during the middle of the summer.

Given what the delegates in Philadelphia wanted to do, it would have been difficult to reach their goals within Congress' direction for the meeting. Simply amending the Articles of Confederation would not do the job.

Madison made sure that wouldn't be the case. He developed a plan that was the basis for early discussions. It didn't merely suggest changes in the Articles; it called for a new document.

Looking back upon that summer of discussion and debate there were three major issues.

One was how a state's population would be weighed in choosing representatives to Congress.

A second was how to establish a strong national government without letting too much power — no more kings! — fall to an individual or a group within the government.

A third was the distribution of powers between the federal government and the states.

HOUSE OF REPRESENTATIVES

Number of Representatives per State based on population.

SENATE

2 Senators per State regardless of State size or population.

There was general agreement at the convention that there should be a two-house national legislature. Also, the framers were willing to let the members of the lower house be elected directly by the people. Disagreement came over how the upper body, the Senate, and the President, called "Governor" at first, would be chosen.

Several plans came before the convention. One, drafted primarily by Madison, came to be called the Virginia Plan or the Randolph Plan. Madison got Edmund Randolph, the young governor of Virginia and an effective speaker, to push the plan in the meetings, thus the name.

Virginia was the largest state. Not surprisingly, the Virginia Plan called for the number of Congressmen to be determined by the number of people who lived in a state. States with larger populations would have more Congressmen.

There was also the New Jersey Plan. This gave all the states the same number of Congressmen. New Jersey, of course, was a small state.

Finally Roger Sherman introduced the Connecticut Plan, better known today as the "Great Compromise."

This was the plan included in the Constitution. One of the two lawmaking bodies in Congress, the House of Representatives, is based on the number of people in a state. This was the convention's recognition of democracy.

The other is the Senate. Each state, regardless of its population, has the same number of Senators, two each. Today Senators are elected by the people in each state. At first they were chosen by state legislatures. The change came with the 17th Amendment to the Constitution, effective in 1913.

Congressmen, members of the House, are elected every two years. Senators serve six-year terms.

The question of how to have a strong federal government but not put too much power in anyone's hands was a difficult one. The brilliant solution came from Madison. He utilized his research, reading, and education — he had attended the College of New Jersey (now Princeton University) — and proposed what we call "checks and balances." It is also known as separation of powers.

Madison's idea was not original. He used what he had seen work in some of the states as well as ideas developed in the books he had read. Although he had his own ideas, he was a good politician. He worked quietly and he was flexible.

It was more important to Madison that the general idea he thought best be approved even if the final result was not exactly what he had proposed. The heart of the checks and balances approach is that power is divided between three parts or branches of the federal government.

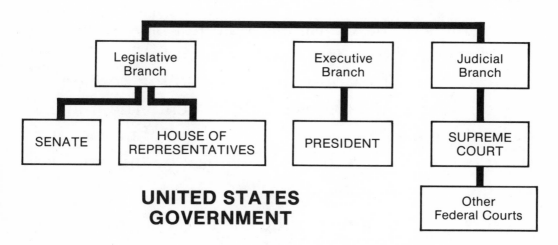

UNITED STATES GOVERNMENT

Article I of the Constitution established the Legislative branch — Congress. It was given the power to make laws, collect taxes, borrow money, regulate commerce with foreign nations and among the states, coin money, establish post offices, declare war, set up and maintain armed forces, and be the lawmaking body for a district chosen as the new site for the federal government — which would be the District of Columbia.

Any law would have to be passed by both the House and the Senate.

Article II set up an Executive branch — the Presidency. Its powers were to see that the laws passed by Congress are carried out, head the armed forces, make treaties with other nations, appoint government officers and judges, including justices of the Supreme Court, and sign (approve) or veto (disallow) laws. The President serves a four-year term.

The 22nd Amendment to the Constitution, ratified in 1951, limits a President to two terms.

The framers of the Constitution did not have enough confidence in the people to allow them to directly elect the President. The Constitution created the position of electors who would choose the President. The framers thought the electors would be their kind of people and stand between a possible "bad" choice by the less informed general population.

Electors were to be named by each state legislature in whatever manner it wished. The number of a state's electors or electoral votes is the total of a state's Senators and Representatives. From the beginning, a state would have a minimum of three electors — two Senators and one Representative. In 1987, six states still had only the minimum of three. California, with 45 Representatives, had 47 electors.

So though most of us believe we vote for a President and Vice President, technically, we only think we do.

We actually are voting for a slate of electors or for individual electors. The procedure varies among the states. The names of the Presidential and Vice Presidential candidates appear on the ballot in most states. Therefore, people think they are voting for the candidate.

In reality a state's electors vote for the President. The candidate with the majority of the electoral votes becomes President.

Under the 12th Amendment, ratified in 1804, the same is true with regard to the Vice President.

As a matter of practice, the electors today reflect the popular vote in their states although the Constitution does not require them to do so.

Therefore, it is possible for someone to lose the popular vote and be elected President. This has happened three times.

Fifteen Presidents have been elected without having won a majority of the popular vote. Abraham Lincoln was elected President in 1860 when he won less than 40 percent of the votes in a four-way contest.

Article III of the Constitution established the Judicial branch including the Supreme Court and other federal courts. The Supreme Court is best known today for its role in determining whether or not a law conforms to the Constitution. This role was not spelled out in the Constitution itself.

The checks and balances are many.

The President has the power to veto a law. Congress can override a veto if two-thirds of the members of each body vote to do so.

The President's right to enact a treaty must be approved by two-thirds of the Senate. Presidential appointments, including those to the Supreme Court, are subject to "the advice and consent of the Senate."

Another check on the power of government is that the members of the House, Senators, and the President are elected and hold office for a limited time. During the Constitutional Convention there was talk of the President and Senators being appointed and holding office for life. Instead voters can choose whether to return an office holder.

The question of how much power the states would retain was also a prickly one. Madison wanted a strong national government, but he wanted it's powers to be "few and defined."

Under the federal system established by the Constitution the states had to share power with the national (federal) government.

The Constitution granted some specific powers to Congress.

Also under Article VI, the Constitution is "the supreme law of the land." If state laws differed, the Constitution prevailed.

Some powers are shared. Both the federal and state governments can levy taxes.

Some powers were denied the states. They cannot print money, for instance.

Some powers were denied the federal government. For instance, goods shipped from one state to another could not be singled out for taxation.

It was presumed that all powers not granted to Congress nor denied to the states belonged to the states. This was guaranteed by the 10th Amendment, ratified in 1791.

Thus states have the right to make laws concerning things relating directly to the people. This includes property and inheritance laws, determining systems of education, establishing voting qualifications, and providing for the recording of vital statistics. Much of this is done today at the local level. The Constitution, itself, makes no mention of local government.

Nor does the Constitution deal with how states relate to one another. Article IV does say the states shall honor other states' laws. It also says a citizen of one state shall be treated by another state the same as would be a citizen of that other state.

This article also gives Congress the right to bring in new states and says the federal government shall protect the citizens of all the states against violence from within or without.

By September of 1787 the delegates had reached agreement and Gouverneur Morris, a delegate from Pennsylvania, was drawing together a document to be published and presented to Congress.

On September 17, 39 of the 42 delegates still in Philadelphia, dipped quills into a silver ink stand to sign the Constitution. It was the same ink stand used 11 years before by the signers of the Declaration of Independence.

The signers included Madison, Hamilton, and Washington. The ever-cautious Randolph did not sign. Nor did Elbridge Gerry of Massachusetts or George Mason of Virginia. The latter two wanted the document to include a bill of rights.

The following day the Constitution was read before the Pennsylvania Assembly. On September 19 it was published in the *Pennsylvania Packet*.

The document published that day in Philadelphia framed the government under which the United States of America would still operate 200 years and 37 more states later.